The 99 Poems of Enlightenment at the End of Knowing

(inclusive of the first two)

by
Ali Khatibi

An absolute treasure trove of punchy divine poetry with beautiful rhyme and rhythm. Each subsequent poem flows deeper and deeper into universal spiritual mysteries, brilliantly revealing them one at a time.

This little book is a poetic shortcut from the temporal to the Timeless. Each poem immediately tackles the next fundamental aspect of spiritual awakening toward a mature conclusion in an appropriate order.

These beautiful rhymes do not waste the reader's time. They are a small collection that firmly and consistently sticks to the point. Each poem stands on its own and provides the topic for a new conversation. Collectively, they are a summary that provide what is perhaps the most rapid journey from person (ego) to presence (abidance) on any bookshelf.

♥

The 99 Poems of Enlightenment
at the End of Knowing

Library of Congress Control Number: 2022905397
ISBN: 979-8-9859906-0-7 (Paperback)
ISBN: 979-8-9859906-1-4 (eBook)

Alismile Ali Khatibi P&B
99poems@alismile.com
www.alismile.com
Washington, DC

The best of names (attributes) belong only to God: Love, Life, Peace, Is, Exists (the only 'I Am'), One, Truth, Self-Sufficient, Timeless, Spaceless, Unbound, Being, Joy, Bliss, Good, Kind, Compassion, Mercy, Grace, Heaven, Holy, Real, Wise, All-Encompassing, Sovereign, King, Majesty, Magnificent, Perfect, Power, Salvation, Savior, Divine, Hope, Constant, Consistent, Spirit, Safe, Sane, Secure, Ideal, Generous, Omniscient, Faithful, Omnipotent, Fabulous, Omnipresent, Incredible, Comfort, Supreme, Confident, Boundless, Inconceivable, Immutable, Everlasting, Dignity, Stable, Light, Lord, All-Knowing, Master, Mighty, Victor, Just, Precious, Refuge, Ruler, Self-Existent, Shelter, Shield, Creator, Wonderful, Fantastic, Free, Excellent, Great, Beauty, Conscious, Aware, Witness, Glory, Praiseworthy, Noble, Delight, Happy, Serene, Tranquil, Subtle, Pure, Honest, Honor, Superb, Splendid, Ecstasy, Fair, Firm, Benevolent, Awesome, Absolute, Actual, Positive, Intimate, Friend, Abundant, Guide, Amazing, Elegant, Glorious, Sublime, Owner, Victorious, Magnanimous, Permanent, Grand, Persistent, Substantial, Exquisite, Pleasure, Paradise, Home, Profound, Innocent, the only Will ...

The 99 Poems of Enlightenment at the End of Knowing

(inclusive of the first two)

by
Ali Khatibi

Table of Contents

In the Glorious Name, Sweet Compassion,

and Loving Kindness of the Merciful God

Introduction

The Lord is my only hope of Salvation

Praise be to God for any True contemplation

Now, it's strictly for the reader to decide

If the poet's inspiration has God as Guide

So, pray keep the scriptures by your side

And let that be how these verses are verified

And, if you find any shortcomings in what you see

Kindly implore forgiveness for me

Dear reader, please take the following important points into account:

It is important to synchronize our vocabulary. In these poems the word 'self' is only used to identify the fake self or ego, and is thus treated accordingly.

In what follows, the reader would also notice that the best and most elevated of attributes (names) are understood to belong only to God, and are capitalized mid sentence in reverence. Thus, the word 'Real' is taken as an attribute of the Divine. Consequently, Really is also capitalized in Really Happy as a Divine level of Happiness, or Really sincere as Absolute sincerity. In Truth, these attributes are not meant to be conceptual. For example, Being prior to the temporal concept of Being, Awareness beyond the temporal concept of Awareness, and so on. This should eventually become clear.

Also, the word 'IS' is at times written in all caps due to being the closest word the poet has that points to the absolute ISNESS of the Almighty.

Also, a mundane point to note is that commas are at times used to assist with pauses in the spoken melody of the verses, and not necessarily for grammatical accuracy.

Finally, at the start, these verses are speaking to the person. Eventually, the words are pointing to Presence.

Prayer of gratitude for Grace

Praise be to Almighty God, the One Unique Lord
Praise be to the Beloved that's ecstatically adored

Praise be to the Self-Luminous Light of the Divine
The Light that transforms a clean heart into a shrine

Praise be to the Divine Light of Being
The One and only Light for True seeing

Praise be to the glow of the Lord's Perfect attributes
Whose reflection, the meaning of righteousness constitutes

Praise be to the Creator of all, that beacons
Whose Grace inspires, enlightens and awakens

(1) To begin with

Ego is a very ensnarling snake
That bites you when you are not awake
And then says listen, this was all a plot
So that the Potter could complain about the pot
Come on then, I'll take you up on high
From there, you could pretend to own the sky
Suddenly a better angel spake
Be careful he said, you will fall and break
And then, once you are finally awake
You'll know this was the poison of that snake

(2) The fall

Here is a mystery that you should fathom
This shattered mirror, is the body of Adam
As one soul we were created, in a garden of Perfection
Embracing God's image, in selfless reflection
When Adam fell, all that was utterly smashed
From the Timeless to the temporal, we crashed

(3) The start of 'me'ing

For Adam to egotistically start 'me'ing
Pretending independence from Being
Is nothing but an illusion of conceit
Based on that liar's original deceit
The simple answer to the question, why?
Is that self-sufficiency for an "image" is a lie

(4) The lie

When a person claims ' I ', it is a lie
Ignore this fact, and you will die
Ego tempts you, to proclaim your 'self'
An idle jest, and a frustrated cry
Forget this world, the Truth is within
If you have a Good heart, God will answer why

---

(5) The fake 'self'

My 'self' is a trap, and pride an absurd notion
Lose not sight of God, in your self-absorption
Do not think thoughts that will disgrace
For your intentions are the shape of your face
When the curtain falls, and Truth is revealed
You will be ashamed of all you ever concealed

---

(6) The strife

As one soul we were created, before this strife
And as one soul we shall return, back to Life
The temporal will end, its demise is fated
When this curtain falls, nothing will be debated
When the chaff is discarded from the wheat
And the bitter is separated from the sweet
The unrepentant haters will be self-indicted
And the Lovers will once again be reunited

---

(7) Intentions

For all your actions and all your deeds

Your intentions are the only seed

In Eternity all is settled and concluded

The temporal veil is drawn and none is deluded

Tis plainly obvious, and not so very deep

What you have sown here, is what you will reap

(8) The illusion

The life of this world is less than, the blinking of an eye

Everything you hoard vanishes, even before you die

This medley of dreams, is but an illusion

Holding on to it, is a mere delusion

All this bother, for things that only perish!

Tis a temporal wisdom, that is Actually foolish

(9) The vanity

Vanity of vanities this world you desperately seek

Lands you without a paddle up the proverbial creek

Another circle and back where you started

Is the destination of the path you've charted

Naked to the temporal you were born

And naked from it you will be torn

(10) Ego's temporal home

Fittingly, the unattainable desire has the temporal as its home

Walk through the old ruins of that arrogant city, Rome

Every wagging tongue silenced, every stone finally crushed low

Tis the nature of the temporal, and thus must needs be so

Blown to the oblivion of the past, and then, dust to dust

All that appears has already gone, oh what a futile lust!

(11) Endless greed

Let the insatiable miser know the end result of his barter

Perhaps this may make him slightly smarter

Every day that his hoard increases greedily

His life becomes shorter and shorter speedily

(12) The deception

Look at the arrogant man who is completely deceived

And boasts gloatingly of the success he has achieved

When the temporal is no longer covering his eyes

And gone is the mirage of this pretentious disguise

Finally, the ultimate joke is on the conceited

The arrogant, are the only ones who will be cheated

What was the gain, bartering his soul for this world

And losing them both, when it was all said and told?

(13) The wilderness

In time, ego's fiction is supported by the neurosis it has amassed

With the inevitable fear of death, it is constantly harassed

That's why it manifests as a worrisome mind

It's another mechanism of the phantom's bind

The 'me' story is only memory, and to that it must hold on fast

Since it's absolutely nothing, in the absence of the past

In the wilderness of time, ego is the serpent, alas

It's only made up of thoughts, so just give it all a pass

(14) The deluded clown

Ego's person, is the clown that jumped in and bowed

It took credit, or blame, and even rowed

The final trap of playing that silly role

Is blindness to the nature of the soul

Thus, realizing ego's absolute irrelevance

Is good reason to treat it with irreverence

Relegate it back to the oblivion whence it belongs

And don't be dragged in by the deluded throngs

Emancipation, is to be freed from that needy clown

Before its melodrama causes the victim to drown

(15) Only God is Self-Sufficient

The promise of pride's fantasy helm
Is to be the master of this phony realm

The temporal is a joke on the fake king
It disappears faster, the harder you cling

Ego is the pretentious liar that's entirely deficient
It is God and God alone, who is Self-Sufficient

(16) Who do you serve?

Didn't Jesus say in Judea, having left Galilee
"Let the little children come to me"?

Didn't he also say, when the very young were at ease
"for the kingdom of Heaven belongs to such as these"?

We are born with the Innocent Awareness of a child
Before this world's deception has us beguiled

Eventually the temporal warps the mind
Into an outlook that is to the Eternal blind

The finite's impulse for miserly greed, has us disgraced
As the Infinite's Generous Abundance, is replaced

The Timeless and temporal are opposites, if you observe
Thus, no soul may both of these masters serve

You will be devoted to one, and the other you'll despise
Though the choice is finally yours, I should apprise

Thus, remember what you are in Reality
And detach from this temporal superficiality

(17) Nothing to worry

Seek the Savior while there is still time
If you waste this chance, it will be a crime
To be alone in darkness is horrific and fearful
Hurry to the Lord repentant and tearful
You'll have nothing to worry, and no reason to fear
Your Father's arms are wide open, if you are Really sincere!

---

(18) Faith is sincerity

If you wish to reach the Highest height
You need not struggle and you need not fight
First in yourself, you must be Truly sincere
Tis the only way, to Honestly think clear
What does your heart seek, what is your role?
Who are you serving, what is your goal?
Are you enslaved by idols, or in search of ideals?
To whom do you plead, and make your appeals?
Do you want your heart to be clean and bright?
Do you only yearn to reflect the Eternal Light?
Faith is sincerity, so let's be very clear
How could you be faithful, if you are not even sincere?

---

(19) The start of True sincerity

Ego is that snake with a deadly sting
It steals from you everything you bring
It lurks and hisses enticements of pride and control
Its ultimate goal is to destroy your very soul
It's the faker and the liar and the cheat
It seeks only to cause your Spiritual defeat
Always engaged in endless innovation
Guaranteed to poison your every motivation
All you say and do is marred with ego's pollution
Its favorite lair is to hide in your perceived solution
An increasingly creative master of conceit
It fools you until your destruction is complete
It promises to amuse and to enthrall
But in fact, it's the precursor to every fall
Now, it's right for you to take the poet to task
What is the conclusion of this story, you may ask?
The secret of sincerity lies in this one clue
Find ego's influence in everything you say and do

(20) We are mirrors

Everything you say and do
Echoes right back to you
If hatred is what you give
Yourself as a hater, you then receive
If Love and Joy is what you reflect
Then that's what for yourself, you must first select
The secret of Peace is to discover
We are mirrors that see ourselves in what's done to the other

(21) The Here & Now

Left to its own device, man imagines the craziest notions
Condemning, hating, and other warped emotions
What's needed is not pain and suffering
It wouldn't be salvation if that was the offering
Trying hard and feeling pain does not suffice
Following your heart in sincerity is not a sacrifice
God is Here with you Now, and this is what you must
Surrender, Forgive, bless, let go, and simply trust

(22) Baptism of Love

Are you a man of God, or merely religious?
Do you yearn to Forgive, or are you litigious?
Love and Forgiveness are together and inseparable
The humble and broken are not irreparable
God's baptism of Love, is an affair that's Spiritual
Tis not a burial in doctrine or ritual

(23) Hidden from the learned

Ego has many tricks up its sleeve
Far too many for us to conceive

See, how the august debate theological confusion
Confidently declaring the correct solution

Each tribe disagreeing with the other's conclusion
Too proud and self-assured to reach any resolution

Oh, for Heaven's sake, could they at least be agreed
That Love is central to their creed?

As to their opinions,
I am not sure Love gives a smidgeon
All religions have Love,
But Love has no religion

(24) The spiritual person's new face

One whisper of the Beloved has made you feel wise
It's only a mere glimpse behind this disguise

Has your ego gone without a trace?
Is everyone admiring your new humble face?

Totally unaware of ego's new chase
You modestly claim credentials in the religious race

You think you understand and now have it all
Your ego even claims this might not be a fall

It's God's Grace that the gift not deserved bestows
It's God's Mercy that the deserved outcome withholds

Don't fall in the trap of the spiritual self
The only one who is not seeing it, is your 'self'

(25) Addicted to attention

What are you offering for attraction to ensue?
What is it that is bringing them to you?

Being the center of attention is a clever snare
It allows ego to feed on every praise and stare

Ego even feigns humility amidst the raves
For the constant recognition it desperately craves

The faithful are Truly modest and unassuming
They fear the danger and the fall that is looming

(26) The golden calf

Half the words we utter are designed to reveal

And the other half are meant to conceal

Tis our ego's idols that decide which is which

When to be honest, and then when to switch

What we sacrifice to those idols, brings us shame

Hiding the scar, is the name of our game

If our disgrace is revealed we become a beast

When this is the one we should confess, at least

What innocence is sacrificed upon that golden calf?

What wrong is done by us, or on our behalf?

(27) Amazing Grace

Fooled by ego's enticements, he was led astray

So, he fell on his knees and started to pray

"Now I know where it all went wrong

Please help me Father, for I am not Strong"

God listens intently, and Compassionately hears

Each dripping sound of a repentant heart's tears

For the Truly sincere, the Lord is Infinitely Kind

Amazing Grace, is all that you'll find!

(28) Thirsty for Life

Rumi saw mankind as a clay jar, with a thirsty cry

Filled with water, whilst its lips are bone dry

If Grace causes the soul to stir

And you die to the you, that you thought you were

What's born again, after breaking that thirsty jar

Realizes the water has always been Here, and not far

(29) In my youth

I imagined flirtations to be Love, and they were not
Twas all dust with which I tried to fill this pot
I entered thirsty, and thirsty I departed
This desert always left me broken-hearted
Knowledge and reason went only so far
Where's the fabled tavern that will fill this jar?
Turn your gaze away from this outward fixation
You are wrong to think Love is a mere sensation
The Truth is not of the world, for you to search and find
Nor will you behold it in the confines of your mind
Love resides solely in a clean and sincere heart
And that is the only place from which you may start

(30) Now that you are here

After all the searching and knocking
The end result was somewhat shocking
Alas, the world isn't such a dazzling place
Finally, no one wins this ridiculous race
You've searched for the Light, for oh so many days
That the temporal isn't as distracting to your gaze
In time God revealed, you should look into your heart
Now, it's Love that will give you the Real start
If ego stops you here, it would be a shame
For tis only True Love that will set you aflame

(31) The promised nation

Are you religiously searching for that promised nation?
Such a realm is not found by outward observation
The kingdom of God is within, you may have heard
You enter through a pure heart, Love hath stirred
You must die before you die, it has been told
And be born again in Spirit, while still in this world

(32) Where True Love (God) resides

You may only fall in Love with Love, and none other
All other ventures, will never be worth the bother
Love only resides in a Good heart, that's clean and sincere
It bestows the Light that makes the unseen clear
If you worship Love's Light, by humble reflection
Then you'll Love all others, with True affection

(33) The best of names

The best of names belong only to God
Be it Love, Light or Joy... all are qualities of God
Of all God's attributes, Love is Supreme
For all the other virtues, flow in Love's stream
Understanding this, is the purpose of one's mind
Those who see it are thus, righteous and Kind

(34) True Pleasure

To see this, you need not be very clever or smart
That the only precious jewel, is a clean and sincere heart
The path of Love is both dignified and upright
Righteousness is its own reward and delight
For any who wish to hear, there is this advice
God and God alone, is True Pleasure and Paradise

(35) This inside out world

The temporal is the reverse of the Eternal
This inside out world, is not something external
Thus, to find the Truth you must look inside
Reality does not in the temporal abide
This makes no sense, you may complain
So, here is an example that might explain
How complex is the world the dreamer dreams
Everything is out there, to him it seems!
Perhaps now you see the wisdom of this saying
Your opinion, it might thus be swaying
Finally, these words of Jesus you may have read
"The kingdom of God is within" is what he had said

(36) The Life raft

In this finite world, so much nonsense is said and done
There are many lies, but the Truth is only One
The temporal drowns you in a sea of confusion
It's the means by which ego preserves its delusion
Love is the Noah's ark that keeps you afloat
Perhaps this is the Spiritual meaning of that boat

(37) Sincerity is not half-hearted

God is True Love and accepts nothing half-hearted
If you are not in Love with Love, you haven't even started
In order not to remain from God apart
You must give to Love your entire heart
Constantly melt in True Love with all your heart
Until there is no one left to be apart

(38) **Tired of it all**

What attribute of this Adam, that's merely "an image", would conspire
To fantasize a willful separate self, as its phony attire
If not some arrogance, that time itself shall inevitably retire?

That's why it's a blessing for the mind to eventually tire
Of its temporal stage that only vanishes, as if on fire
And thus let go of the mind's fake self, as an unattainable desire

---

(39) **The temporal mind's veil**

What more could the mind ever bring
Other than some other imagined thing?
The Inconceivable is not something for the mental self to find
With the promise of yet another concept from the mind
The Unbound, by definition has no form
Thus, the Formless is merely veiled by that mental storm
How could the Imageless be imagined by the mind
When Truth is not some 'thing' that the mind could find?

---

(40) **What's behind the veil?**

Without the veil of believing, conceiving, or imagining how
The Truth is already Spacelessly Here, and Timelessly Now
First to find out what you are, be still, you are not far
If it's perceived or conceived, it's not the perceiver that you are
But Now realize, even that perceiver is being Witnessed, and by what?
What's reporting the perceiver and conceiver that's not?

---

(41) The Blessed Bliss

What does the sincere seeker miss
If not the Beloved, that is pure Bliss?
Until from within, a sacred kiss
Dissolves the seeker, in a Blessed Bliss

(42) Beware of the thief

The Unbound is not some finite place, and thus not far
The Spaceless is where you already are
The Boundless isn't another image to be shown
Nor is the Timeless some mental thing to be known
Thus, every image and thought upon the Beloved, is a veil
Don't get lost on that temporal trail
Mental knowledge, is a memory that's already stale
Subject to forgetting, thus vulnerable and frail
The Absolute actually Exists and IS, always Fresh
Not a prisoner in the net of memory's temporal mesh
The poems that follow try to expand on this
And help stop the mind from stealing Freedom's Bliss

(43) Let's start with the initial trap of ego

Initially, ego is attention presuming a 'self' upon thought
And the turmoil this misassociation has brought
The mental story of a false self, that it thus carves
Is only thought based, and without thought it starves
The prodigal is lost in thoughts, hence the Truth is not far
So, cling not unto thoughts, to be left with what you are!

(44) Ego's mental bind

For those who are asleep, ego is its own hell
God willing, this poetry is the wake-up bell
In order to put this menace behind
Realize ego is what a person calls my mind
Also, tis a jumble of thoughts that are sensed as a mind
And ego is nothing more than a mental bind
Using thoughts, ego makes its false claim
Pretending personhood, is its ultimate aim

So long as the illusion is maintained, that some person chooses
Ego doesn't care if the fake self wins or loses
Thus, ego is equally propped up by approval or shame
Either vanity or self-loathing feeds it, exactly the same
Ego could claim personality with thoughts of hatred or vanity
And even think itself into a state of total insanity
Thoughts may thus become that serpent's poison tongue
A person is that mental bubble, and is already stung

So, please wake up and start getting a clue
And see what harm ego's person could do
What follows is hopefully a big slap
To wake perception out of this mental trap
Wisdom is preserved in what age old sayings say
In understanding the message that they relay
Wisdom is brutal towards such thought
"Never mind" is the saying, when advice is sought
A person is seen as fake, so very obviously
That it is declared, "stop taking yourself so seriously"

Taking the mind seriously is totally absurd
For any thought has passed, since it's already occurred
Thus, thoughts are merely memories of imagination
Why then get sucked into their mental intimidation?
Memories are tombstones in the graveyard of the past
Thus, thoughts are mere phantoms ego has cast
So, don't believe the role mind pushes you to play
Be the detached Witness, and in the Truth stay

(45) Freedom

Mind is like a glass upon the mirror of perception's eyes
On it ego paints all manner of lies
Ego uses enticements, to make you crave
It warps your mind, and then turns you into a slave
It sits inside your mental hat
With thoughts of having this and being that
It distracts you with yet another shiny thing
And then uses fear to administer its next sting
It threatens that, only in the temporal you may abide
And thus saddles you and takes you, for yet another ride
It says you should by this world be defined
So that you are in its fading fiction confined

Don't be reduced to such a pathetic role
And stop climbing the temporal's greasy pole
For ego to hide behind these masks
Your attention is all that it asks
To regain Awareness, end this crazy distraction
By understanding the futility of its attraction

Ego uses thoughts to whisper in your ear
It hisses, "if I die in silence, so will you my dear"
So, if you want to be free of the ugly little creep
Look away from thoughts, don't even take a peep
Deny that serpent the oxygen it needs
Disregard all the thinking on which it feeds
Relax and allow it to slowly die
Quiet your mind and be still, if you want to fly
End all the turbulent chatter and worthless grief
Enjoy the deep Peace of Silence, with a sigh of relief

(46) Before the start of when

Soon as you were born, before the start of when
Who exactly were you, right there and then?
When you were still innocent of all thought
Gladly observing what fate had brought
Before you even knew someone had given you a name
When boy and girl to you were exactly the same
Before the distraction of the story of me
What was it that you could clearly see?

A clear consciousness unsullied by form
Reflecting Pure Awareness, was your True norm
Think about that time, for a little bit
Twas just before duality started the mental split
Then, the temporal distracted your gaze
Blurring your perception, with its growing haze
The Timeless, was veiled by labels and notions
And all the other temporal poisons and potions

Fortunately, you don't have to go back in time
To wash away years of worldly slime
Irrespective of what the world may claim
You did not change, when they gave you a name
Forget your 'self' if you want to be free
Remove the shadow of thought, to once again see

To again be conscious of the Awareness that has always been
Go behind the person and this temporal scene
Forget identity, nationality and sects
Drop all words, thoughts, forms and objects
Detach and let go of this world's tiresome task
Find out what is left without the ego's mask!

(47) Beyond the usefulness of mind

Give your heart to the Captain of this ship
Don't allow your mind to push and make you slip
Throw the serpent of thoughts overboard
Unburden the weight of all you've ever stored
Discard the frustration of want and desire
Set it all aflame, and burn it in the fire

Intellect will only bring you to the door
Then it's silence that will take you to the core
Thoughts and words will only describe the sky
But it's on Love's wings with which you fly
If you only listen to the mind
Then information is all that you'll find
Alas, thoughts conceal what silence shows
The mind informs, but it's the heart that knows
Don't confuse the mind's map with the Actual place
Know who you are, and perceive by God's Grace
You are pure consciousness, empty of this world
If you see this, the temporal will lose its hold

When the Lord says "I AM", this message is sent
True Being, is neither an object nor just an event
The Spaceless is not a 'thing', to be sought and caught
Nor will you behold the Timeless, in some passing thought
Let go of the arrogance of your presumed will
Trust, submit, surrender, and be still
In the selfless Silence of mental stillness, you may find
What you'll never know by the thoughts in your mind

(48) The Safest stance

This world is something you should barely watch
Do not take on the color of everything you touch
The temporal is upon the Timeless, merely a veil
Everything finite, will by definition fail
We say this world is in time, because it only disappears
Holding onto it will thus, leave you in tears
So forget the world, it's not worth a dime
Leave the prison of space, and the shackles of time

If I were to ask, who are you my friend?
Pure consciousness, is what you might contend
Well done, that is both correct and clever
Now look deeper, who is Witnessing the observer?
A mirror may only see through the eyes being reflected
At One with that Truth, when selflessly connected
If you become the reflected image you were meant to be
Then once again, you'll start to see
To be only conscious of Awareness, is a clue
Enjoy that silent Peace, and allow it to stew

Let the righteousness in your heart constantly grow
Stay as you Truly are since before the veil, long ago
Take refuge in the ark of God's Love, in your heart
And stay from the noise of this world, apart
Then watch the temporal pass you by, from a safe distance
Tis but a fading mirage, without any substance

(49) The Intimate One

The only intimacy is with God, and God alone
The Majestic Lord of a clean heart's throne
All plurals are merely temporal fodder
In Truth there is literally no 'other'
Reality is binary with two numbers to count
God is number One, and zero is man's amount

To reflect on this, unclutter the mirror of perception
Discard the temporal's distractions and deception
And be sure to appreciate this simple admission
A mirror may only reflect in selfless submission
So, ignore the arrogance of ego's construction
Your 'self' is to the mirror, but an obstruction

Now, what is left to perceive other than Awareness
Tis the closest companion, in all fairness
Awareness is an attribute of God, and is as Light
It allows the soul to perceive and have sight
And what is it to be alive if not, to be Aware?
It's the only constant in perception's stare
So, there is absolute submission to Awareness, just to be alive
Thus, for submission, there is no need to strive

Now the soul which is merely a mirror, has shown
God's Light is the only One that's intimately known

(50) The story of me

Flowing down a strand of hair into the sea

Is a droplet of memories I call me

Memory strings up ego's claims on that strand of hair

In time, it withers and dies no matter how fair

Perhaps a few pictures might hold that thin thread

Perchance remind someone when the mask is dead

Without a string of memories you lose all the beads

Of the story of me and its fragile needs

Me, is just a flimsy thought, don't you see?

Without memories, there is no me

(51) You are not a story

I hope we may reach a consent

That you are not merely an event

Drop the fake self's false claims and theories

You are not the content of your memories

Building a shrine to the past is madness

It will only sink you in deeper sadness

Don't let thoughts cast a shadow on your heart

And keep you from the Truth apart

Of what does the appearance of this world consist

Other than a future and a past, that do not Exist?

(52) The separate person

There is no separate person, there is no me
The story of me, is just a story, don't you see?
A story is not the Being, and will never last
Tis a mere memory, in the graveyard of the past
Why suffer to pretend some silly separation?
Puffed up with pride or held together by desperation
To end the slavery of propping up the fake me
You need only drop the pretense, to break free
Absolutely ignore the person, and give it no slack
Once you knew Santa isn't Real, he didn't come back

(53) Pretense or Presence

Ego's enticement of a willful, separate 'I'
Is the false promise, of that first lie
The unattainable nature of that elusive desire
Is the ungratified taste of its frustrated fire
Ego weaves a web of stories with a frightful skill
Like a spider trapping its prey for a final kill
Entangled as its own web, the fake self does not see
Arrogance, is the story of a self-sufficient me
Witness your 'person' as some actor on some stage
Acting cool, getting emotional, or showing rage
Whether preparing those lines, or in character saying
Ultimately, you are not the role that you are playing
Integrity starts with being true to this fact
There is no need to pretend and continue this act
Ego uses memories and thoughts in order to conceal
That humble dignity comes from staying Real
My person is a prisoner of time and stories amassed
It consists only of memories buried in the past
Reflect only God's Truth in Timeless Presence
The unassociated Being that is the One True Essence

(54) This dream's end

He asked "who are you Really?", and there was an empty gap

For my ego that blank instance was a big slap

That question's answer I did not know

Suddenly, there was no 'me' for me to show!

Ego shrieked its presumed will, and started to flip

"Mind, define that concept for me, and get a grip"

Suddenly, mind put on its thinking cap

Oozing notions and concepts to cover up the empty gap

But wake up, that is finally it, my friend

That blank instance is Actually, this dream's empty end!

The temporal and its finite forms disguise ego's futile trap

Where Formless seems empty, and Timeless a blank gap

---

(55) So this is the fake mask!

Ego is self-aggrandizing, as you expect from the sleaze

Dignity is self-deprecating, and ready to please

Ego's mask is a hurricane of you should, I would, and desire

The melodrama of concepts and judgments, colors its attire

In the hurricane of 'me', I asked who am I and why?

When I got to the eye of my storm, there was no 'I'

In that stillness, consciousness could finally see

In the absence of melodrama, there is no 'me'

(56) Not restricted by form

Silence is the only speech
And a quiet mind is what will teach
Thoughts could only imagine a shape
Don't partake in that poisoned grape
Don't get involved in mind's new spat
Arguing about that, when Being is not a thing, to be a 'that'
Don't listen to thoughts, for some hair to split
Trying to explain it, when Love is not an object, to be an 'it'
Observe that mind is only talking to the mind
This subtlest role is the one to find
It continues pretense with this subtle game
The seeker/finder role is one and the same
Both Consciousness and Awareness, the mind will try to fake
To save that fake self, every attempt it will make
To be free of this mental agitation
Don't get involved in its conversation
Be the uninterested observer, that this game sees
And let all thoughts just pass, like yet another breeze
If thoughts paint the image of an even subtler shape
Know the Witness is Formless, from that there is no escape

(57) The silence of surrender

The bad odor that's finally stinking
Is that thoughts won't get rid of the thinking
Thoughts were used as a twig to dislodge the stick
Now throw both away with this final kick
To end this endless substitution condition
The only answer is Absolute submission
When there is no surrenderer making a stand
Silence and surrender go hand in hand

(58) Behind the veil

What is Life that animates the tapestry
Of this creation with all its artistry?
A temporal curtain covered with patterns and shape
Veils the same Timeless Being like a thick drape
Some form is named a bird, another the shape of a tree
One pattern is called you, another identified as me
Life is Life in all forms, and is not just hers or his
A Constant sense of Being, that simply IS

(59) The Absolute ISNESS of God

This finite world is unattainable at last
For nothing separates future from past
Thus relax, there is no need to cling
When in Permanence, there is no 'thing'
So, what is the Unchanging Actuality
The Unassociated Essence that is Reality?
The only Constant we all share
Is the Witness, with an unflinching stare
The Witness within, that all this is seeing
Is a sense of Presence, perceived as Being
Timeless, Spaceless, Formless ISNESS
For it's only IS that IS, and IS the Witness

(60) Succumb to God's Awareness

Now beware of the trickster's usual trick
Lest you get stuck there, for it's still pretty slick
The seeker too is merely a story, and a role being played
It's just another apparent self, and that too must fade
So, remain the detached observer of ego's old trap
For it's the fake self thinking, that the fake self, it will scrap
Treat with appropriate disinterest, this silly deception
Reflect only the Being of God, to preserve proper perception
To that which the mirror of perception reflects, it'll succumb
The image of its True attention, the mirror must needs become

(61) The most Obvious

Let's start with the most obvious fact
What you call the world, is a vanishing act
The future is merely the next past
And thus, the temporal does not last
This finite world is a passing wind that blows
You'll always be surprised, how fast it goes
What is it that Remains, and sees it going?
Where is the Witness, that is Always Knowing?
The seeker says, once I get it, I'll be much better
But, who is observing, even that fake getter?
What is watching the seeker, chasing its tail seeking?
Who is Aware of the presumed 'me', that is speaking?
In order for the mirror of perception to reflect and see
The Light of Awareness, must Always Be
The next point is important, so forgive this one time
If what comes next is not going to rhyme
The Awareness perception is looking for
Is the Awareness perception is looking with!

(62) There is only One Will

Only God Exists as Truth, and all else is vanity
A separate self, is ego's arrogance and insanity
Let's start by being clear about what is known
So as to be wise about the seeds being sown
The future is the next past, thus the temporal is vanishing as time
In this disappearing freefall, what is there to climb?
In the graveyard of memories, lies the story of my personality
Truth is the Timeless Now, there is no rehearsal in Reality
When everything vanishes, what is there to lose?
When there is no person, who is there to choose?
Thus, if this message is understood, stay silent and still
For ego is the frustration, that there is no personal will

(63) So Easy!

What did all this temporal conditioning teach?
That you must work hard and strive, to get and reach
The wisdom of God is foolishness to the world
Spaceless is the opposite of finite, Truth be told
You are already filled with God and free
Soaked within, like a sponge that's in the sea
God is closer to you than the mask of your face
In Reality there is no time and no space
By being nobody, the wise have succeeded
To hold nothing and be nowhere, no effort is needed
The Unbound is so intimate, there is nothing to conceive
It's thus so easy, that it's hard to believe

(64) Distracted from the Truth

It is only with distractions that ego's pretense extends

Beguiled by this temporal mirage, the fake self pretends

With worldly riches, ego entices the fake king

You just keep grabbing, and see what the end will bring!

Ego's promise, is the temptation of the original liar

It all evaporates as 'time', for an unattainable desire

Only God, the True "I AM", is One Self-Sufficient Being

Behind every eye, the same exact Awareness is seeing

In order to perceive this, throw away all notions

Just for once, drop all concepts and negative emotions

Let go of all judgments and confrontations

Don't think what's next, and end all expectations

Give up the melodrama of the story of me

Forget your fake self, and for one moment, be free

If the mind is Truly silenced of its annoying sound

Then the Lord's Presence may be readily found

Now close the eyes, and reflect upon the All-Seeing

Isn't within a sense, that Here is a Formless Being?

Could it be so easy, obvious and clear

That in the absence of distraction, the Truth is so near?

God IS Always Here, so the Beloved is taken for granted

But with temporal distractions, the fake self is so enchanted!

(65) In Truth

In Truth, there is no step to take
In Truth, there is no leap to make
In Truth, there is no seed to sow
In Truth, there is no 'thing' to show
In Truth, there is no time to flow
In Truth, there is no 'where' to go
In Truth, there is no form to constrict
In Truth, there is no space to restrict
In Truth, there is no effort to make
In Truth, there is no test to take
In Truth, there is no thought to find
In Truth, there is no mind to bind
In Truth, there is no future or past
In Truth, there is no first or last
In Truth, there is no wait or when
In Truth, there is no next or then
In Truth, there is no separate will or intention
In Truth, there is no anticipation or tension
In Truth, there is no concept to conceive
In Truth, there is no need to believe
In Truth, there is no word to say
In Truth, there is no role to play
In Truth, there is no want or need
In Truth, there is no lack or greed
In Truth, there is nothing to achieve
In Truth, there is no reason to grieve
In Truth, there is no task to fulfill
In Truth, there is no philosophy to instill
In Truth, there is no ritual to do
In Truth, there is no me or you
In Truth, there is no person to sustain
In Truth, there is no separate ego to maintain
Didn't Jesus say to you and me
That the Truth will set us free?
The substance of which the Truth consists
Is Boundless Reality that Effortlessly Exists

(66) The mirage of memories

Run towards a mirage, and it evaporates away
The temporal world, works in exactly the same way
Whether working hard, or trying to have fun
Towards the next event, we constantly run
The apparent happening of an immediate event
Is the evaporating past, that to memory is sent
So, other than memories, that are merely thought
What else was there that this world constantly brought?
Thus, everything about the temporal we desperately sought
Was the vanishing mirage of an unattainable thought
Now, pay careful attention to the following text
There is some good insight in what's described next
Since every event, is merely temporal evaporation
Of an earlier desire, replaced by the next expectation
Isn't it an addiction, chasing after the next fix?
That's how the temporal veil allows for ego's tricks
Distraction from the Timeless by some temporal stream
Is ego's story of a separate me, as an unattainable dream

(67) Real Trust of the Absolute

'I' is a silly prison with only one bar
Tis ego's story of me as its main star
An illusion of memories, set on an evaporated stage
Tis but mere thoughts that construct that mental cage
Thus, it's important to understand
The largest mirage, doesn't even wet a grain of sand
Since, tis the transient taken seriously, that whispers all of this
Ignore passing thoughts, and give it all a miss
That's why, Real trust of the Absolute
Is the annihilation of the temporal me, in the Timeless Truth
So, why not just drop that original lie?
Ignore the fiction, and let the phantoms die

(68) Misassociation

Ego is a distraction of perception, ergo
Anything paying attention to other than itself, is ego
Misassociation with the temporal, is the start of 'me', as a story
Of shame and defeat, or pride and pretentious glory
But, the temporal vanishes and thus, the story doesn't stick
More distraction is needed, to prolong this trick
The 'person' is hard work, and once that pretense has begun
It becomes the nauseating tale of an endless rerun
Those repetitive thoughts are called the mind
They are ego's phantom person, and tie perception in a bind

Any exposure of this fickle posturing, and ego starts to run
It is a shadow of distraction, and the Truth it must shun
Keep it superficial, don't get so deep, or else I'll flee
Since the end of 'my' story, is the death of 'me'
But, if perception's attention returns to itself, there is hope
To see that the poisonous snake works more like a rope
Attention is what grabs onto distraction's rope
And presumes a person getting dragged down mind's slope
If there was no interest in what thoughts were selling
There would be no story for the mind to be telling
Interest is the hook at the end of mind's projected fishing stick
If intrigued, an otherwise passing thought may click

Every event and thought, has already passed
To the abyss of oblivion, any temporal hook is cast
Do not misassociate as the phantom of a reverse projected thinker
Mind is but a dead corpse in the past, hook, line, and sinker
If indifferent, attention is no longer caught
Without interest, there is no reason to give it a thought
Clouds of thought may come and go in unassociated seeing
When detached all that IS, IS the beautiful day of Being
Disregard the temporal, and the Timeless will show
Mind couldn't rope 'you' back in, if there is no 'you' to let go!

(69) The dream projector

Upon every statement being told
The mind, an image of it does mold
No matter how subtle or elevated words may be
Thoughts are painting an image, for the mind to see
The shapes formed are all a mental block
Wherein the phantom of the fake self is stuck
So, imprisoned in a finite illusion
Mind is the projector of its own temporal delusion
That's why words have never found
The Spaceless and Timeless that's Unbound
Tis Grace upon a pure heart that must needs unwind
The confinement of ego's mental bind

(70) The phantom fight

The egoic mind is the phantom of the self, that's fake
Thoughts are seen as Real, by mistake
Ego's pretence feeds on conceptualized resistance
Even as the frustration of pointless persistence
The only way to salvage what's at stake
Is to eliminate that elusive fake
That phantom, is the only one fighting the mind
So, leave that fake fighter behind

(71) No thought

The marketplace of the unattainable is fraught
With the advertisements of thought
And the veil that a sense of separation has brought
Is merely the length of any thought
But the Unbound is far beyond the confines of thought
Only Existence Exists, what's there to be sought?

(72) The mirror of perception

Pure consciousness, is an image of its attention

It's a reflection, on the mirror of perception

Why then focus on this worldly veil?

Why suffer by assuming this finite jail?

Look away from the dreams of the temporal night

Turn the mirror of perception upon God's Light

To reflect the Timeless, it needs be told

A mirror was not made to take and hold

A mirror is meant to only reflect and give

You must be empty of all form, to once again Live

Forget your presumed self, to be what you ought

God is the True One, and man is naught

---

(73) How Sweet

How sweet is God, better than any friend

The only intimacy, without beginning or end

A Graceful Father, who patiently Protects and Guides

A revelation that keeps revealing and never hides

Always Here, come sunshine or rain

Intertwined, like sugar in sugarcane

---

(74) Are we two?

The temporal keeps repeating, still its arguments are seldom new

The actors' masks may differ, but the tiresome stories are few

It's thus important to ask the question, what am I, and who?

Nothing in the temporal lasts, are any of ego's claims true?

But, if it ever becomes obvious that in Love there is no me or you

That identity is only a temporal story, and thus we are not Really two

Then the one who Truly Forgives, does not even exist to blame

True Forgiveness is thus Sublime, because it makes Absolutely no claim

---

(75) Forgiveness

Love is not a thing to find

Truth is not a concept defined

All concepts are mentally confined

Thus, Freedom is beyond the mind

That's why in order to be Truly Kind

The words gently uttered are, "never mind"

---

(76) The unknowing

Grace is the flowering of God's Presence in the mirror of perception

All that IS, is the Lord's Gracious reception

The separate seeker and knower is another veil

It's the arrogance that has become stale

'Known' is a concept recorded by 'me' as past

The past is non-existence, that to oblivion is cast

For the mirror 'me' is an unattainable desire

That is why 'ego' is frustration's painful fire

So, there is no person and no 'me' to be shown

That Truth is not contained in what 'me' has known

There never was, is, or will be a 'me'

A fake self, the Truth will not see

There is no other authority independently listening and seeing

Only Existence IS, and all that IS, is Being

When the separate self is revealed as fake, with no 'where' to hide

The mirror is only surrender, with God as Guide

Thus, here is something to finally admit

When there is no 'me', who is there to submit?

An image-bearing mirror is already total submission

That is the original nature of its created condition

(77) Without 'me'

Without 'me', no fake pretends in every conversation
Without 'me', no pretense projects a person for every sensation

Without 'me', there is no opinionated point of contention
Without 'me', there is no one to feed another performer's pretension

Without 'me', there is no actor playing a part and seeking attention
Without 'me', there is no futile melodrama for this pretense's extension

Without 'me', there is no need to imagine an identity with some intention
Without 'me', there is no prisoner in the bubble of a trapped perception!

(78) Gifts of righteous annihilation

Tis only Freedom that frees, not a person
Tis only Seeing that sees, not a person
Tis only Perceiving that perceives, not a person
Tis only Receiving that receives, not a person
Tis only Discerning that discerns, not a person
Tis only Returning that returns, not a person
Tis only Grace that bestows the seer, not a person
Tis only Love that draws near, not a person
Tis only Light that enlightens, not a person
Tis only Life that enlivens, not a person
There is no ego living life, that gets and gives
The Bestower is Life alone, since only Life Lives

(79) Stillness before a response

When a tense conversation has started, stop!

The itch for an instant response is only ego, let that drop

Allow surrendered sincerity to let in the Light

So that the seeing is cleared and bright

And then, God willing, delight in the surprise

When the right counter question, does arise

And if ego is not indulged, and to the extent it dies

All are drawn closer to that Gentle Prize

What in a sage question, that friend might recognize

May be the Light within, which is far more wise

---

(80) Little to say

If a question is asked, respond with all sincerity

Submit to the Holy Spirit, and observe all charity

Otherwise, if not pressed on righteousness or morals

Why get involved in any temporal quarrels?

The one without an identity has little to say

The games of pretense, the selfless do not play

When there is no argument, the words are very few

When there is no point to view from, where's the point of view?

(81) ISNESS

IS, is the only One that sees it all

Every rise and every fall

Mind could only imagine a 'thing' that has been

The mind and all of its 'things' are seen

Every 'thing' that is thought or shown

Is not the Awareness to whom it's known

(82) Return to the image

In Truth the Greatest number is One

Beyond the All-Encompassing, there is none

If this mirror is once again God's image, in selfless reflection

It would presume no identity, or separate intention

If the arrogance of 'myself' is forever gone

Then who is left other than the One?

(83) Love is the Oneness of Being

God's image, we were meant to selflessly reflect

An independent mirror, has no image to detect

Union in Love, is a fruit of selfless submission

Tis the only way to correct the human condition

Worship and reflection, are one and the same

The true worshiper has no 'self' to claim

If you mimic an Ideal, that's what you've become

There is no distinction among those who succumb

True Lovers are reflecting the same exact Light

Selflessness is their path and their final delight

(84) True Silence

Ego is the phantom that thinks it has a say
When it all just goes on anyway!

It imagines it decides and sows the seeds
A phantom doer of an illusion that does the deeds

A measure of how much ego's person is deceived
Is that oddly, thoughts have already occurred, when perceived

Simply ignored, the temporal vanishes, and won't even get to have a say
So, why should silly thoughts distract, and have their way?

Thus, when a passing thought tries to have a sway
Surrender the fake doer, and just let the temporal fade away

Not trying is ego's absolute abyss
So then, just give it all up, and let all those arrows miss

Unwelcome thoughts are ego's nasty game
True surrender and silence are one and the same

(85) Surrender the seeker

What say does a mirror have upon the image selected?
What claim does a soul have on the light reflected?

Awakening is not bestowed on ego because it has striven
In Truth, it is ego that veils the gift of Life that is freely given

For the undistracted mirror there is no seer, only seeing
There is no person living, just Life and the One Being

Salvation is not a prize for ego's next rat race
So, surrender that surrenderer to God's Grace

(86) The obstacle

Dear friend, these verses are all bidden

To reveal what ego's 'I' has hidden

To do this let's first drop my personal story

And only sing praise of the Beloved's Glory

Praise be to the One Being, in my being

The One that's Seeing, even my seeing

The True Presence, that's in my presence

The very Essence, of my essence

Now Let's see why humility is the key to salvation

And the freedom that's in self-annihilation

Without me being, there is only Being

Without me seeing, there is only Seeing

Without me present, there is only Presence

As me slowly lessens, what is left is the Essence

And that is why the sages say

It's only you that's in the way

(87) So, where was Adam thrown?

Initially, from Adam only an "image" of the Spaceless was Being shown

If the fall was from the Timeless, then where was Adam thrown?

To start with, an "image" is that which has no identity of its own

But if a different identity, is the unattainable seed that was sown

Then Oneness was lost, and from it many finite masks were known

And to the temporal wind, that arrogance was blown

(88) The axe that cuts the noose

Personhood is like the rope that binds up perception

It's ego's ultimate weapon of pretentious deception

My 'self' is a pretense based on playing some role

It's a distraction from Truth, that blinds the soul

Call it ego or person, it's all the same thing

Both are the venom of the exact same sting

Thus, the person is not something that would mend

From pretense to Presence, is this journey's end

So finally, let's get down to brass tacks

And cut down that noose with the following axe

Real Peace is not the peace of the person

Real Peace, is Peace from the person

Real Freedom is not the freedom of the person

Real Freedom, is Freedom from the person

Real Salvation is not the salvation of the person

Real Salvation, is to be saved from the person

(89) Epitome

To once again reflect upon God's Glory
Let's return to the genesis of this poetic story
Ego is the apple a mere creature should not bite
It's a warping of perception that distorts its sight

Adam was created to be an "image" of God's Perfection
But beware, an "image" is only a surrendered reflection
Reflection is humble submission, not vanity
Pretending a separate self, is arrogant insanity
Also, an image's identity is not up for selection
It is predefined by the subject of its reflection

What is worship, if not reflecting an Ideal?
Without submission, how could a mirror reveal?
A willful mirror is but a frustrated dream
In time, its futility becomes a torturous scream
Thus, the fake self must needs be crucified
There is no way my pretentious 'me' could be justified
The elimination of 'me' ends the inevitable pain
Removing ego's mask is the ultimate gain

Finally, the meaning of this song is not in the words of the singer
Words are merely pointing, and thoughts only see the finger
God is not some finite idea to be conceptually defined
The Timeless and Spaceless could not be verbally confined
There is neither an adequate word nor a temporal seeing
Truth Absolutely IS, and Love is the Boundless Oneness of Being

It is only as an "image" of 'Being', that a reborn Adam could Be
It's only through the reflected Eye of God, that Adam could See
Thus for an "image", a different identity is a lie and an original sin
There is no separate person to See the 'Being' within!

(90) Final warning and the original trick

If you've understood what is said so far
Avoid ego's original trick, don't forget what you are

Don't confuse perception's mirror with the Actual Light
Many fall for this, the distinction appears slight

To claim Self-Sufficiency, is ego's greatest lie of all
Cloaking pride in religion, facilitates the fall

A mirror has no claim on the Light it reflects
God's Grace bestows, and God's Love selects

Be humble and cringe, if you are ever praised
Give all credit to the Lord, and you won't be fazed

---

(91) Why silence is golden

The undistracted Presence of God's Being, makes the heart flutter
The most eloquent description, is but an inadequate mutter

Substance is the gap between words, all else is noise and clatter
Presence is revealed in silence, all words are merely chatter

Even a single word uttered, is far too much said
The Truth is Life Now, but a verbal concept is dead

In the clarity of silence, undistracted by a single word
All that IS, is the Being of the Presence of the Lord

---

(92) Addicted to definition

Mind is the addiction to temporal definitions

And all of its inherent restrictions

Reality could never get defined

Since the Unbound isn't confined

Description is limitation, by definition

Thus, the Unlimited defies description

---

(93) The sage's final words

The point to which all this poetry is reduced

Is to expose the idea that has Adam seduced

For the mind, something is seriously amiss

The Truth it seeks, is a mental abyss

The Spaceless IS, Unbound beyond all restrictions

Thus the Beloved IS, prior to all descriptions

The Timeless, which IS prior even to silence, is by the temporal unstained

That for which one word is too much said, is not explained

Mind has no oxygen at this altitude

There is no use anymore for its aptitude

Since, this is how Truth is beyond the end of the mind

The Witness of thinking, the thoughts themselves will never find

And thus, Here is the end of what the mind has produced

The deduction, is the final distraction to the deduced

That's why at the end, in order for the sage to show

He says, Now throw away all you've learned and know

(94) Gratitude

Be synchronized with God, in humble gratitude
And be blessed with a positive attitude

Simply saying thank you, does not suffice
Gratitude is the surrendered heart, to be precise

This is what humility is Actually stressing
Joyfully make the most of every True blessing

---

(95) The taste of Heaven

"Gratitude is the wine for the soul", Rumi conveyed
"Go ahead, get drunk", no price needs be paid

God is the only Truth, and it's understood
Only Truth Exists, nothing else could

Reality is Boundless, there is no limit
Get higher and higher, there is never a summit

Wouldst that all knew the Timeless Pleasure
It's Never-Ending and without measure

Flooded with gratitude, for what has been found
An ever increasing Joy, that is most Profound

---

(96) Attar's seven cities of Love

They say the cities of Love are seven
The stepping stones on the path to Heaven
Tis the road wise men of old had trod
In order to get closer to God
The first step on this journey knows no rest
A constant search for the city of quest
Second, starts the message from above
To be purified, enter the city of Love
Third, worldly knowledge notwithstanding
The next stop, questions finite understanding
Fourth, leaving all temporal attachment
You are entering Unbound detachment
Fifth, you find the opportunity
To come upon the city of Unity
Sixth, repeating Lord God be praised
What you see now leaves you amazed
Seventh, is the final salvation
In the realm of self-annihilation
Now that God has made the mirror so blessed
The soul is Home Free and able to rest

(97) Dear reader

By myself, I'd only fail and only fall
I'd be dead, if God had not answered my call
If in Ali you are not totally disappointed
Any Good you see is what God has anointed
It would be arrogant for me to make any claim
All praise belongs only to God, and also all the fame

Final Note:

Dear reader,

I hope you enjoyed and have benefited from the poems you read here.

Best Wishes and God Bless,

Ali Khatibi

Printed in Great Britain
by Amazon